The ref has the toss up.

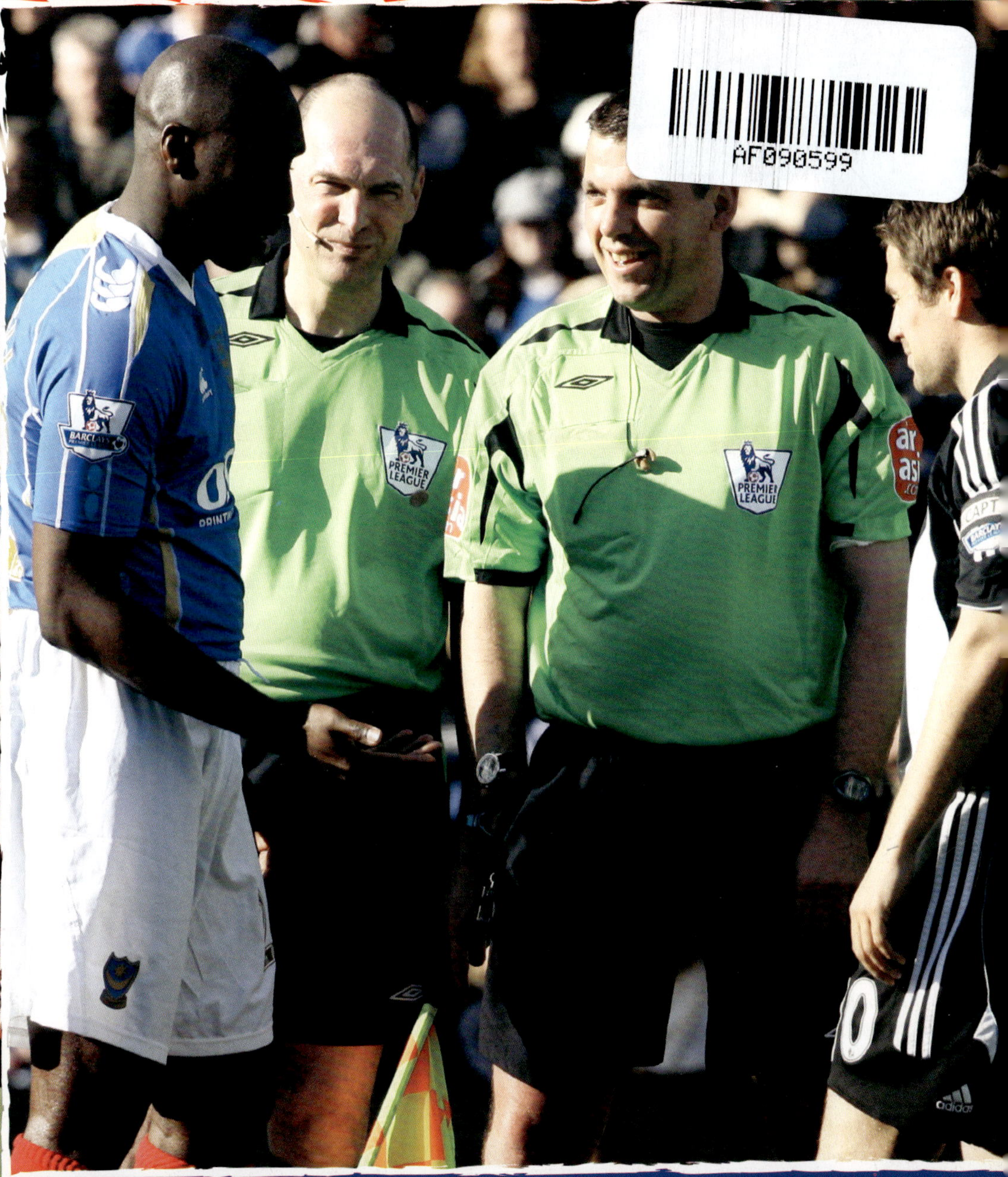

We win!

Kick off!

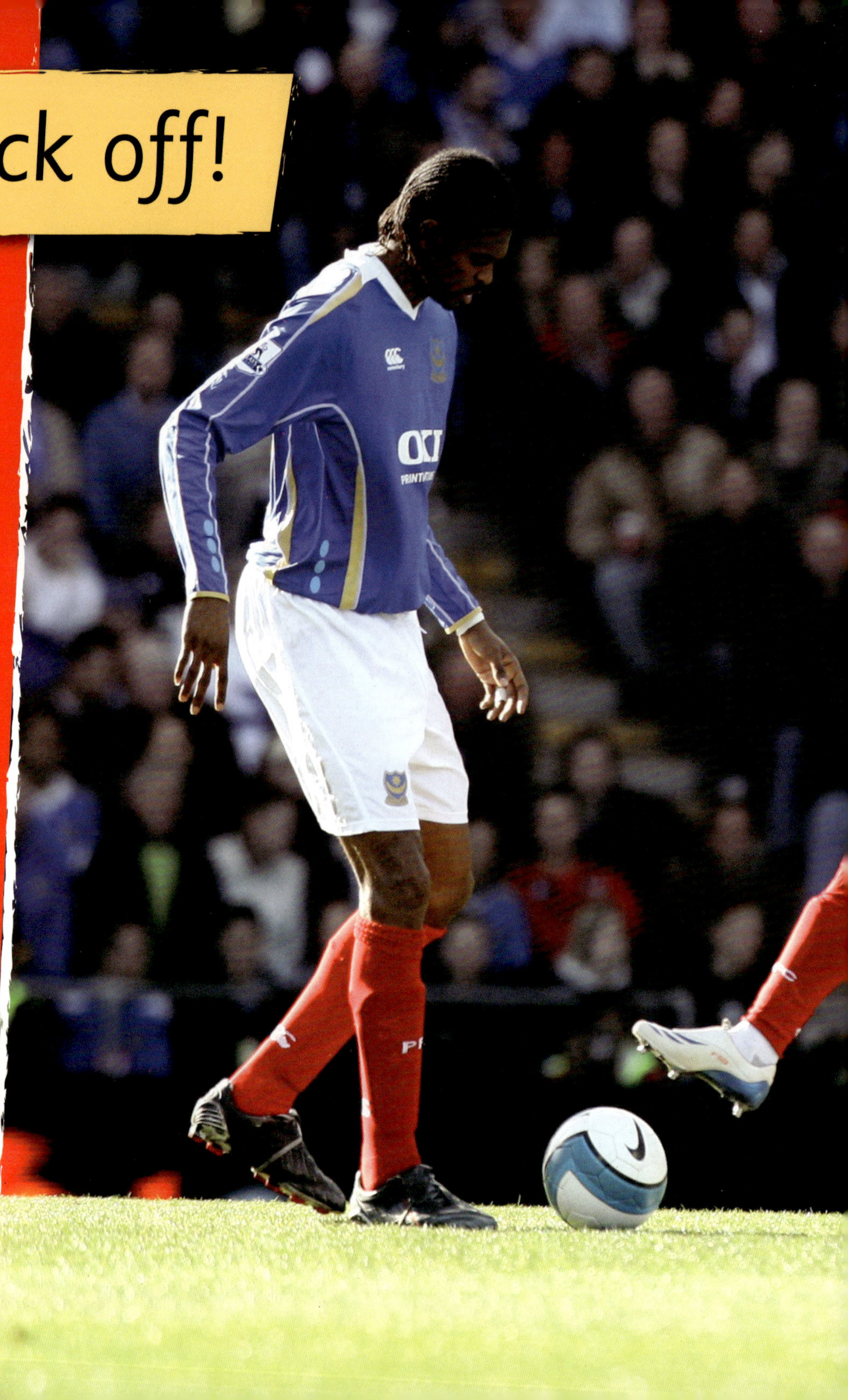

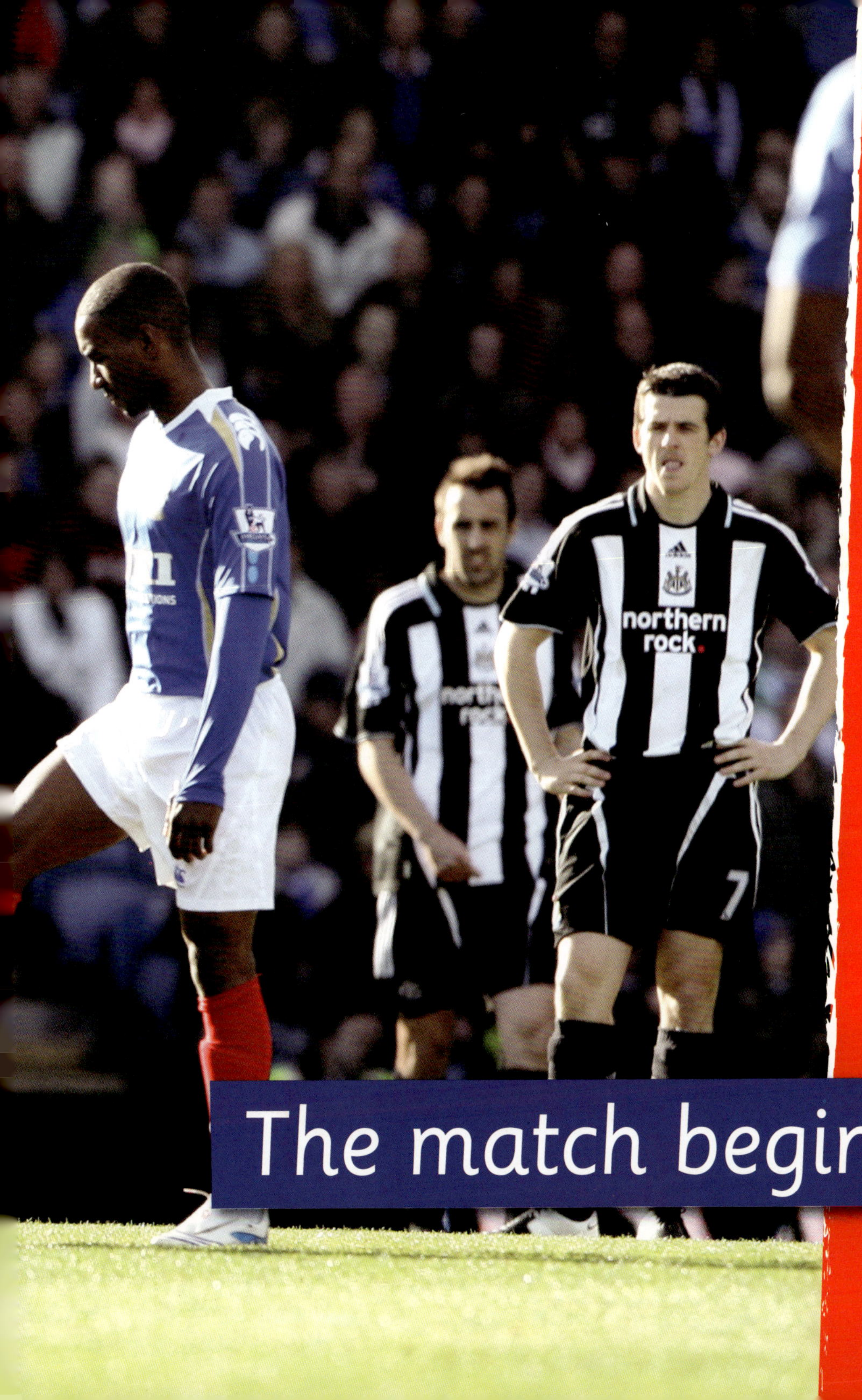

The match begins.

Run!

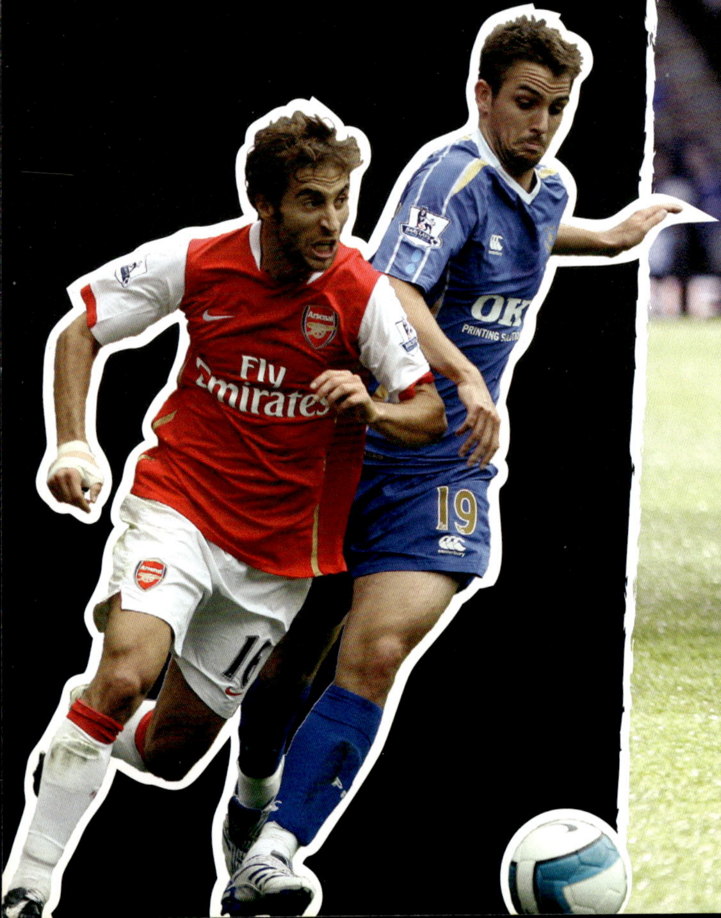

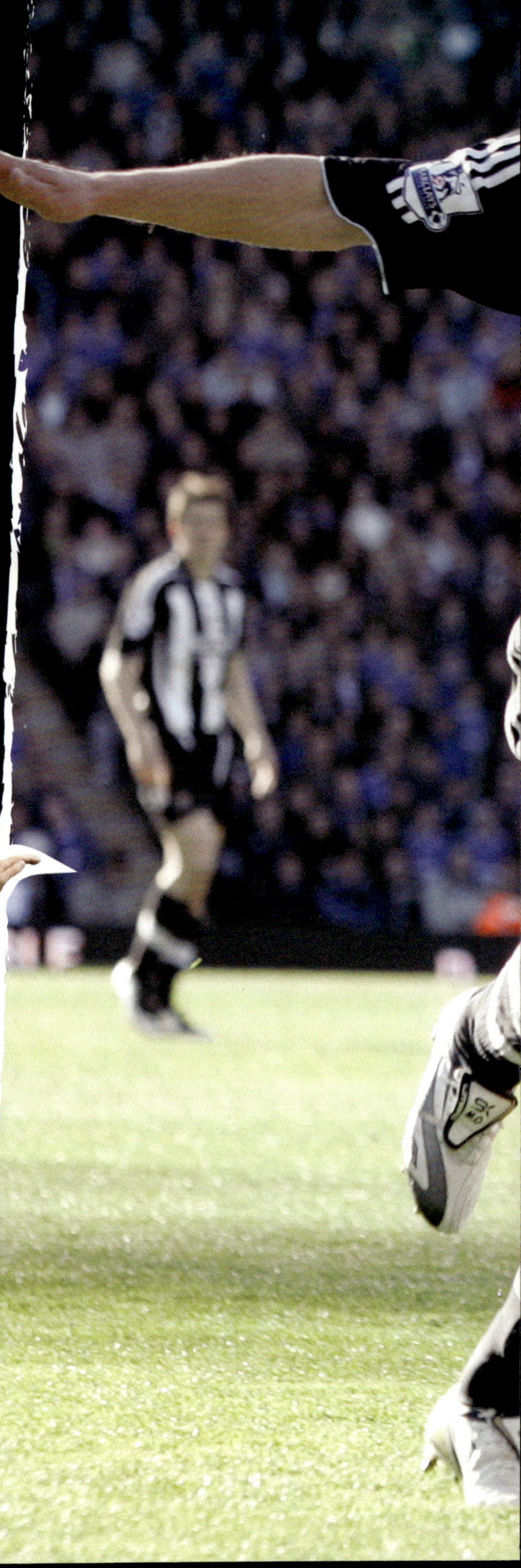

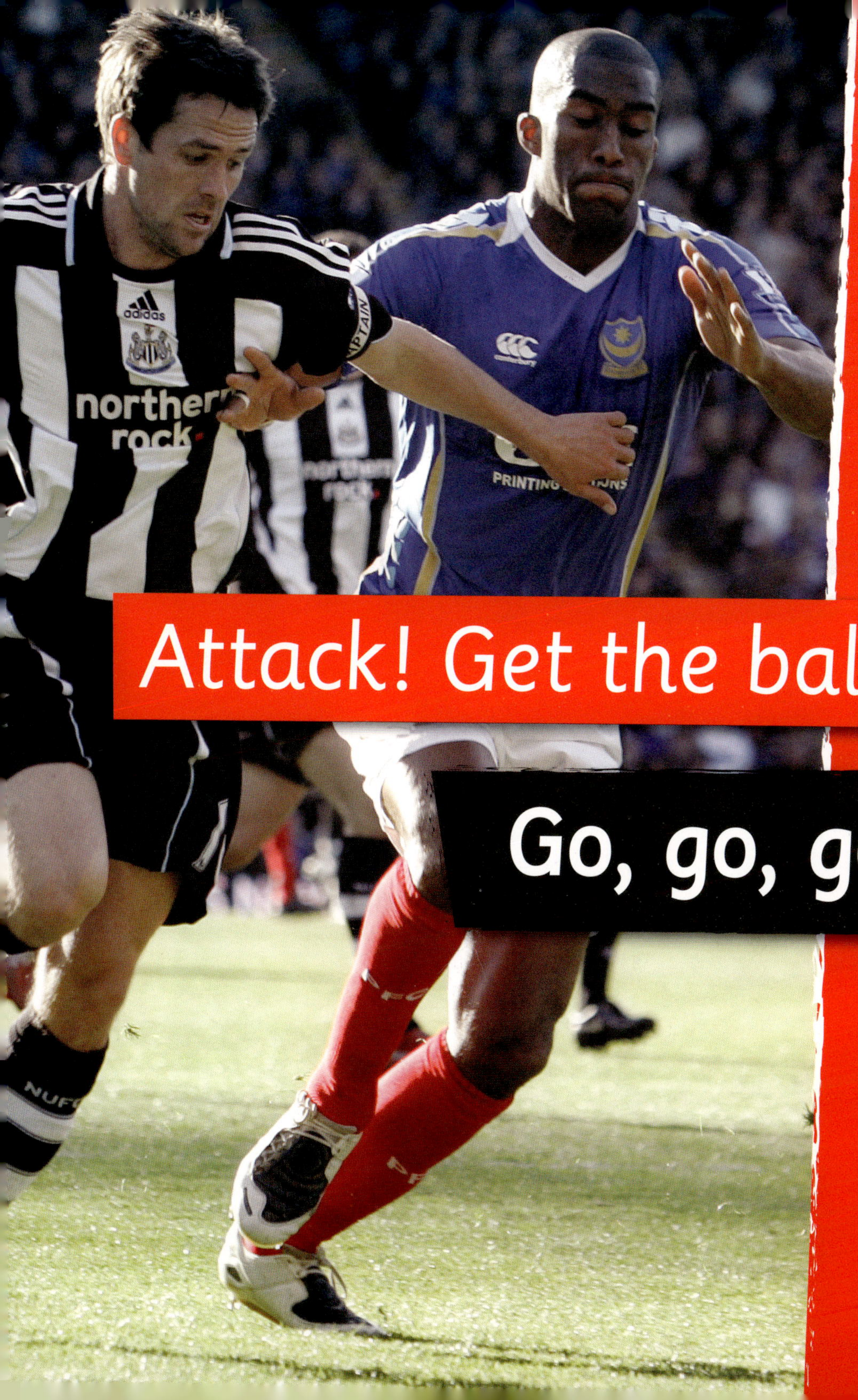

Attack! Get the ball!

Go, go, go!

Run, but no tugs!

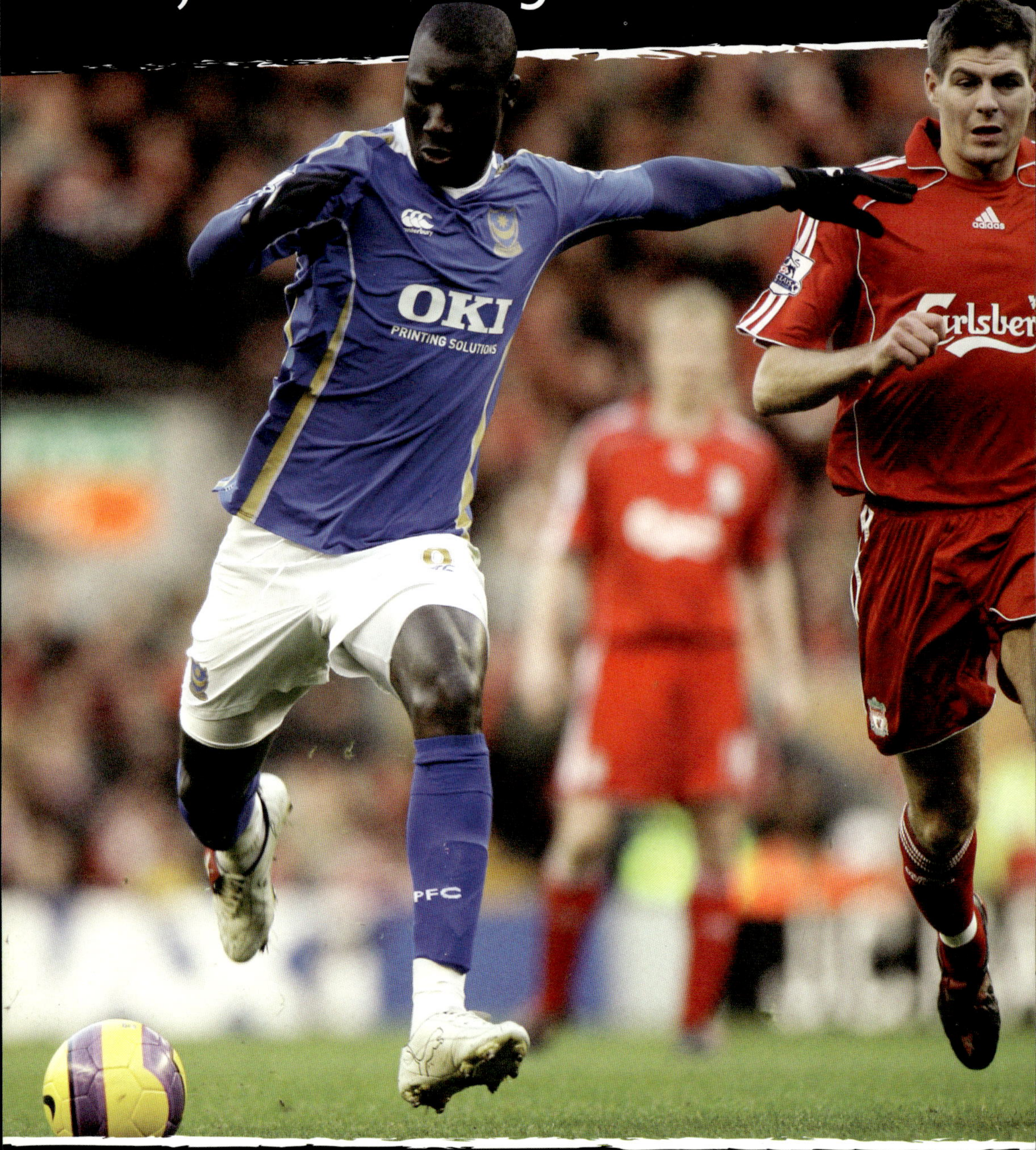

Hit it!

Kick the ball …

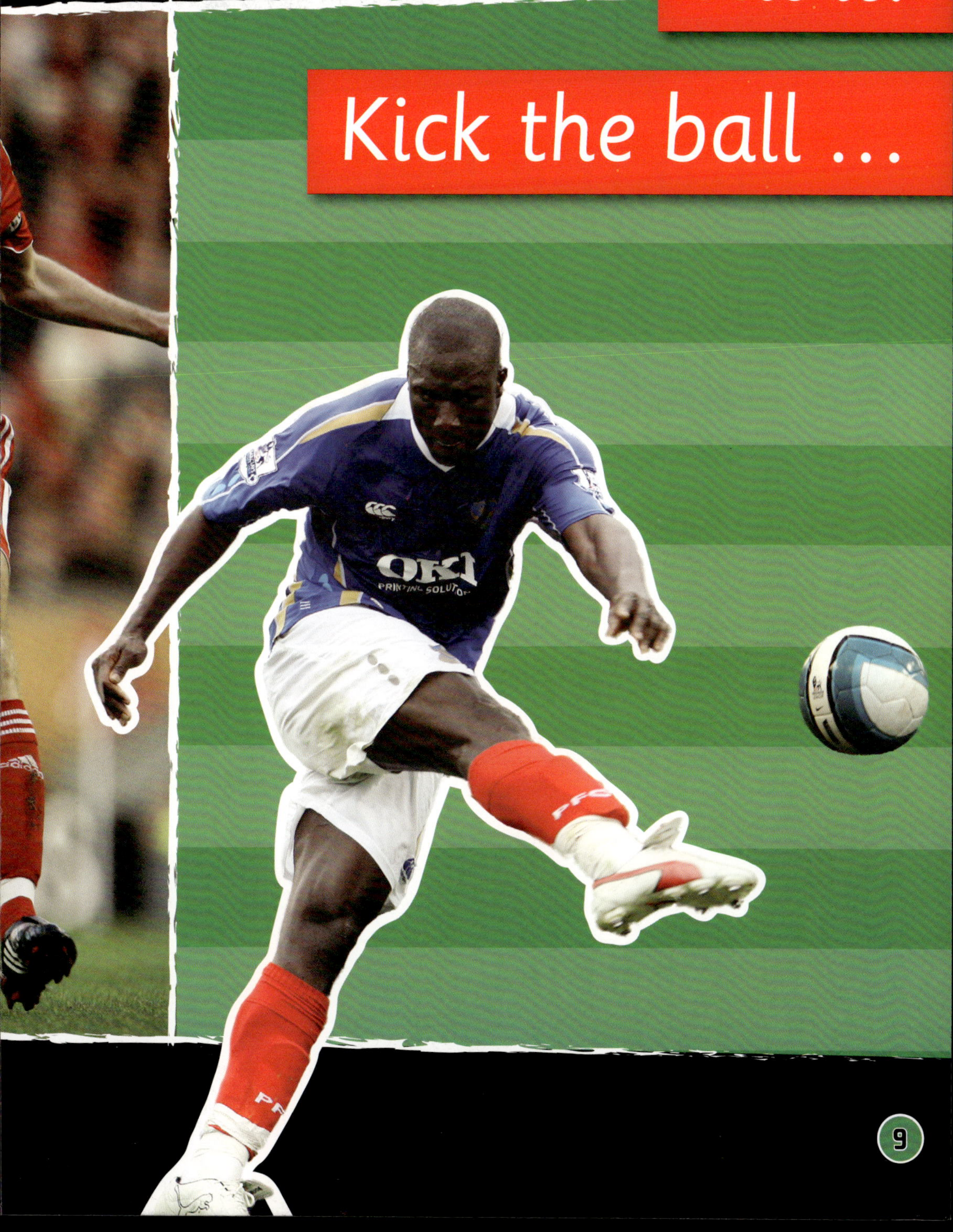

... into the net!

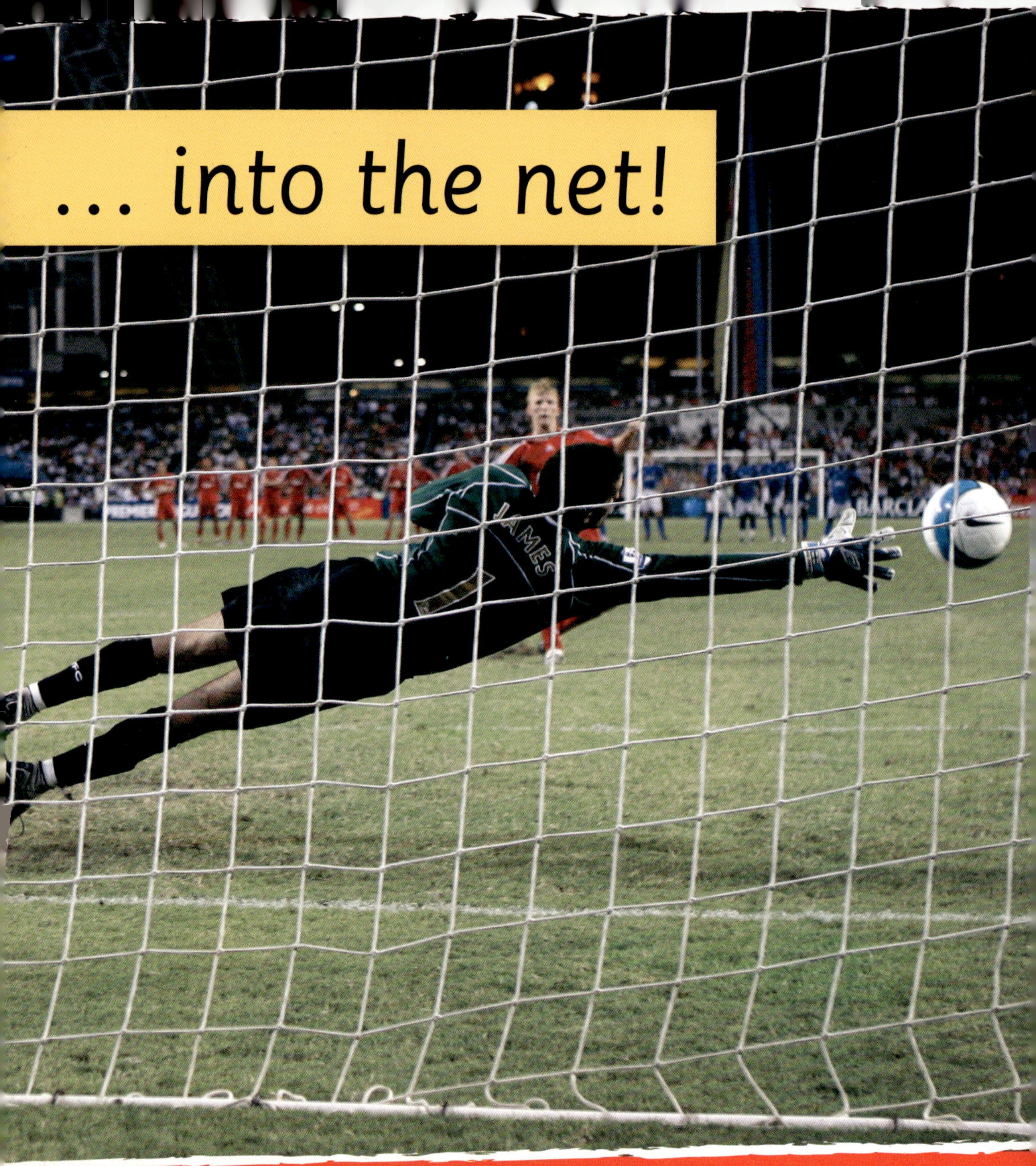